Bones

Injury, Illness, and Health

Revised and updated

Carol Ballard

**Heinemann Library,
Chicago, Illinois**

www.heinemannraintree.com

H Visit our website to find out more information about Heinemann-Raintree books.

To order:

☎ Phone 888-454-2279
💻 Visit www.heinemannraintree.com
to browse our catalog and order online.

Edited by Andrew Farrow, Adrian Vigliano, and
   Pollyanna Poulter
Designed by Steven Mead and Geoff Ward
Original illustrations © Capstone Global Library Limited 2003
Illustrated by David Woodroffe and Geoff Ward
Picture research by Ruth Blair
Originated by Heinemann Library
Printed and bound in China by CTPS

13 12 11 10 09
10 9 8 7 6 5 4 3 2 1

Second edition ISBNs: 978 1 4329 3416 3 (hardcover)
                      978 1 4329 3429 3 (paperback)

The Library of Congress has cataloged the first edition as follows:
Ballard, Carol.
  Bones / Carol Ballard.
    v. cm. -- (Body focus)
Summary: The human skeleton -- Healthy bones -- Types of bone -- Bone structure -- Bone marrow -- Broken bones -- Bone diseases -- Different joints -- Inside joints -- Joint problems and injuries -- Knee injuries -- Arthritis -- Joint replacements -- Spine -- Looking after your spine -- Spinal problems and injuries -- Skull -- Ribcage -- Arm and hand -- Leg and foot.
Includes bibliographical references and index.
  ISBN 1-40340-194-2 -- ISBN 1-40340-450-X (pbk.)
  1. Bones--Juvenile literature. [1. Bones. 2. Skeleton.] I. Title.
II. Series.
  QP88.2 .B35 2003
  611'.71--dc21
                      2002014427

Acknowledgments
The author and publishers are grateful to the following for permission to reproduce copyright material: Corbis pp. **7** (Kevin Fleming), **22** (Stockmarket/Tom and Dee Ann McCarthy), **25** (Stockmarket/Lester Lefkowitz), **41** (Stockmarket/Phillip Bailey); Photolibrary p. **15** (Blend Images); Science Photo Library pp. **5** (Manfred Kage), **6** (Maximilian Stock Ltd), **10**, **12** (Prof. P. Motta/Dept. of Anatomy/University "La Sapienza," Rome), **14** (Dept of Clinical Radiology, Salisbury District Hospital), **16** (Alfred Pasieka), **17** (Biophoto associates), **20** (Peter Gardiner), **23** (Dept. of Clinical Radiology, Salisbury District Hospital), **26** and **34** and **37** (Dr. P. Marazzi), **28** (Mike Devlin), **29** and **35** (Princess Margaret Rose Orthopaedic Hospital), **30**, **38** (Gusto), **39** (Mauro Fermariello), **42** (Pasieka).

Cover image of an X-ray of a hand reproduced with permission of Science Photo Library (George Mattei).

We would like to thank David Wright for his invaluable help in the preparation of this book.

Every effort has been made to contact copyright holders of material reproduced in this book. Any omissions will be rectified in subsequent printings if notice is given to the publishers.

Contents

The Human Skeleton 4

Healthy Bones 6

Types of Bone 8

Bone Structure and Composition 10

Bone Marrow 12

Broken Bones 14

Bone Diseases 16

Different Joints 18

Inside Joints 20

Joint Problems and Injuries 22

Knee Injuries 24

Arthritis 26

Joint Replacements 28

Spine 30

Taking Care of Your Spine 32

Spinal Problems and Injuries 34

Skull 36

Ribcage 38

Arm and Hand 40

Leg and Foot 42

What Can Go Wrong with My Bones? 44

Find Out More 45

Glossary 46

Index 48

Words appearing in the text in bold, **like this**, are explained in the glossary.

The Human Skeleton

The skeleton of bones provides a strong framework for the rest of the human body. It defines our shape, protects important organs, and allows us to move. It also plays an important role in blood cell production and in storing **minerals** and fats.

The skeleton of a newborn baby may contain as many as 300 bones, but many fuse (join together) during childhood. Most adults' skeletons have 206 bones. The bones range in size from the tiny, delicate **ossicles** of the ear to the long, strong **femur** of the thigh. There is also a wide range of bone shapes, including the long bones of the limbs, short bones of the wrist and ankle joints, flat bones of the skull, and irregular bones of the spine and face. The size and shape of each bone reflects its function.

Support

The spine provides a strong, upright central support. The shoulders are attached to the spine by strong muscles, and the **pelvic girdle** is attached directly to the spine. Arms are suspended from the shoulders, and legs are suspended from the pelvic girdle. This arrangement defines our overall shape and the movements that we can make. Bones protect delicate internal organs from injury. The skull protects the brain, the spine protects the **spinal cord**, the ribcage protects the heart and lungs, and the pelvic girdle protects abdominal organs.

Movement

Muscles are attached to bones by strong **tendons**. When muscles contract, bones are pulled into new positions, allowing us to achieve a wide range of movements. Some movements are large, such as the movement of the femur when we stride, while others are small, such as the precise movements of a violinist's fingers.

Joints are the places where the ends of two bones meet. Your skeleton has more than 200 joints. Some joints, like your knees and elbows, allow the bones to move. Strong bands called **ligaments** hold these joints together, controlling the movement of the bones. Other joints, like those in your skull, are fixed, so the bones cannot move at all.

At the center of some bones is spongy **tissue** called red **bone marrow** that produces some blood cells. Adult bones also contain yellow bone marrow tissue. If we eat more fat than our bodies need, the excess will be transported by the blood to places where it can be stored. Some fat will reach the yellow bone marrow, where it may be stored and then released when required by other parts of the body. Bone tissue stores minerals, especially calcium and phosphorus, that help to make the bones strong. When these minerals are needed, bones can release them into the bloodstream to be transported to other parts of the body.

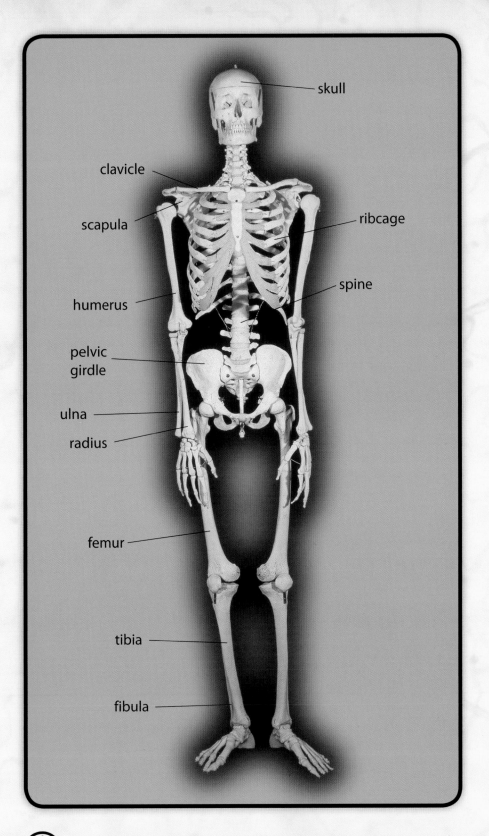

skull

clavicle

scapula

ribcage

humerus

spine

pelvic girdle

ulna

radius

femur

tibia

fibula

This diagram shows the main bones of the human skeleton. You can see how the spine provides a central support for all the bones of the upper body, and the pelvic girdle acts as a frame from which the legs can move freely.

Healthy Bones

We all need to make sure that we take care of our bones, because a strong, healthy skeleton is important if we are to lead active lives. The food that we eat and the amount of exercise we get can both affect our bones.

Diet

Our bones are made from the chemicals that we receive from our food. For bones to grow strong and healthy, we need to make sure that the food we eat provides all the chemicals that are needed by our bones.

Bones contain a lot of calcium and phosphorus, so it is important that your diet contains plenty of these two minerals, especially while you are growing. Smaller amounts of other minerals, such as fluoride, manganese, iron, and magnesium, are also needed. Good sources of calcium include dairy products, such as milk and cheese; leafy green vegetables, such as cabbage and spinach; shellfish; and eggs. Foods rich in phosphorus include dairy products, meat, fish, beans, grains, and eggs. These foods also contain plenty of the other minerals needed.

Some **vitamins** are essential for building strong bones. Vitamin D, found in fish oils, butter, and eggs, and also formed by the action of sunlight on skin, is needed to help calcium build up in the bones. Vitamin C, found in most fruits and vegetables, but especially in citrus fruits such as oranges, also plays an important part in building up strong bones.

Eating a balanced diet helps to build strong bones.

Exercise

When you exercise, your bones are made to move and support your body's weight. This helps them to become stronger as more minerals are accumulated. Being inactive can lead to bones becoming weaker, as minerals are lost and bone tissue is broken down. The main work our bones do is mechanical, being pulled by muscles when we move and supporting our body against the pull of gravity. Weight-bearing activities such as walking and moderate weight lifting help to build and retain bone **mass**. It is important when you are a teenager to build up as much bone mass as you can. As people age, bone mass is lost and cannot be built up again—so the more you have to begin with, the better!

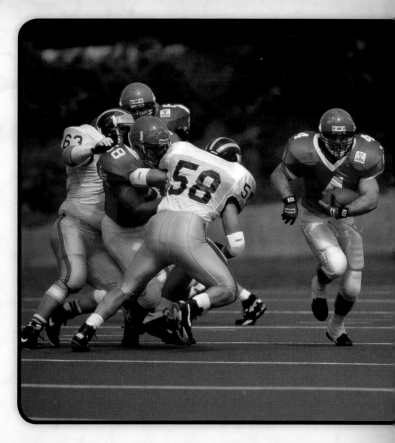

Astronauts and bones

Scientists have discovered just how important exercise is for healthy bones by studying what happens to the bones of astronauts who spend a long time in space. Without the pull of gravity, the human body is lighter. This means that when exercising, the bones do not have to work so hard. The bones begin to lose calcium and other minerals, and even taking extra minerals as pills cannot make up for this.

If you are playing a sport in which you might injure a bone, try to protect yourself by wearing the correct protective clothing. Football players are unlikely to suffer damage beneath all this padding.

HEALTH FOCUS: Protection

Bones can repair themselves, but it makes much more sense to avoid damaging them in the first place! Many sports activities have protective clothing specially designed to protect bones—shin pads for hockey and football; helmets for cycling, horse riding, and mountaineering; and elbowpads and kneepads for inline skating. Football players in particular are extremely well padded and protected.

Types of Bone

The shape and size of bones varies, depending on their functions within the body. Large, strong bones like the thighbone are needed for supporting the weight of the body, while smaller, delicate bones like the ossicles inside the ear carry out tiny, precise movements. Bones are usually grouped according to their shape.

Long bones

Long bones have a greater length than width. They usually have a slight curve that makes them stronger than they would be if they were perfectly straight. There are special places on the long bones where muscles are attached. The bones act as levers and move when they are pulled by the contraction of muscles. The femur (thighbone) and **humerus** (upper arm bone) are examples of long bones.

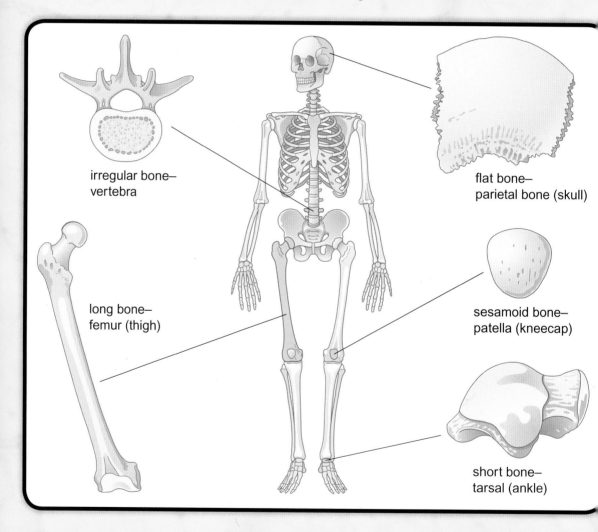

irregular bone—
vertebra

flat bone—
parietal bone (skull)

long bone—
femur (thigh)

sesamoid bone—
patella (kneecap)

short bone—
tarsal (ankle)

These diagrams show some of the main types of bone that make up the human skeleton. A bone's shape is determined by its function. The bones of the spine must surround and protect the spinal cord, so they fit together tightly and have a hollow center. The femur must support the weight of the body, so it is long and strong.

Short bones

Short bones are roughly cube-shaped, with their length, width, and height being almost equal. Carpals are short bones found in the joints of the wrists, and tarsals are short bones found in the joints of the ankles. These bones allow flexibility as they slide easily past each other.

Flat bones

Flat bones are thin, curved, and strong. Their strength makes them ideal for forming spaces to protect organs. Examples of flat bones are the ribs, **scapula** (shoulder blade), **sternum** (breastbone), and some bones of the skull.

Irregular bones

Irregular bones are complex shapes that do not fit into any of the other groups. The **vertebrae** and facial bones are all irregular bones. They have strange pieces jutting out from them that allow them to connect with muscles and other bones.

Sesamoid bones

Sesamoid bones get their name because they are the shape of sesame seeds, although they are a lot bigger. They are found in joints where there is **friction** and tension between tendons and bones, such as the palms of the hands and soles of the feet. The number of these small bones varies from person to person, but everybody has the two large sesamoid bones that we call the kneecaps (patellae).

Accessory bones

Accessory bones are small, extra bones that occur in some people, most often in the feet. They arise when developing bones do not fuse (join together) completely to make a single bone, and so they can look like broken bones on X-rays. This can make it very difficult for doctors to accurately diagnose injuries to bones in the feet.

IN FOCUS: SUTURAL BONES

Sutural bones are accessory bones found between the joints of the bones in the skull. When a baby is born, the skull bones are separate, like jigsaw puzzle pieces that are not fully locked together. As the baby grows, these bones slowly fuse to make the strong dome that we call the **cranium**. The joins between the bones are called sutures, and small sutural bones may be present between the sutures. Because the skull bones do not always fuse together in exactly the same way, the number of sutural bones can vary from one person to another.

Bone Structure and Composition

Bones are not simple solids. They are made of living tissue arranged into several different layers with nerves and a blood supply. Their structure gives them strength, while keeping them as light as possible.

Approximately 70 percent of bone material is made up of different minerals, including calcium phosphate and calcium carbonate. The rest of the bone material is a network of living fibers and bone cells. It is the mineral content of the bone that makes it **rigid**. A baby's bones are quite soft, and young children's bones are still slightly flexible. As people grow older and as more calcium, from the food they eat, is added to the bone structure, the bones slowly become more rigid.

Types of bone cells

There are three main types of bone cell:

- **Osteocytes** transport nutrients, waste, and gases to and from the blood vessels.
- **Osteoblasts** make new bone tissue so that bones can grow and damage can be repaired.
- **Osteoclasts** break down old bone tissue to release minerals.

The actions of these cells are finely balanced. To maintain healthy bones, it is important that bone tissue is not broken down faster than new bone is produced.

Spongy bone has a mesh-like structure that makes it strong and supportive.

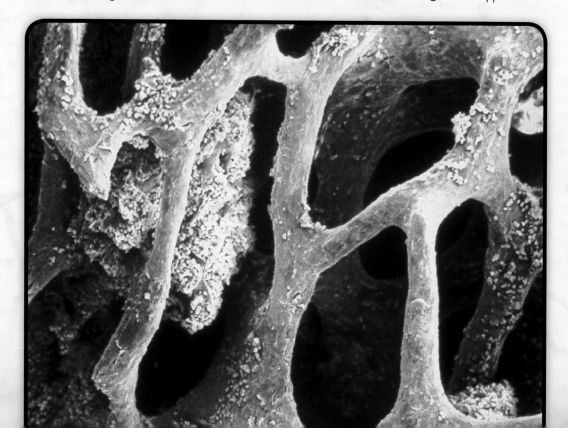

Inside bones

If you look at the inside of a long bone such as the femur, you can see several different areas. The long, cylindrical central part is the shaft (diaphysis). At each end of the shaft is a growth plate (epiphyseal disc), where osteoblasts make new bone tissue, making the bone grow longer. The outer ends of the bone are covered in a layer of smooth **cartilage**, to allow the bone to move freely at the joint.

The outer covering of a bone, the periosteum, is a tough, fibrous **membrane**. It contains osteoblasts, and blood vessels and nerves run through it.

Inside the periosteum is a layer of dense, **compact bone** similar to the ivory of elephants' tusks. It is a network of bony columns, arranged around central canals through which arteries and veins run.

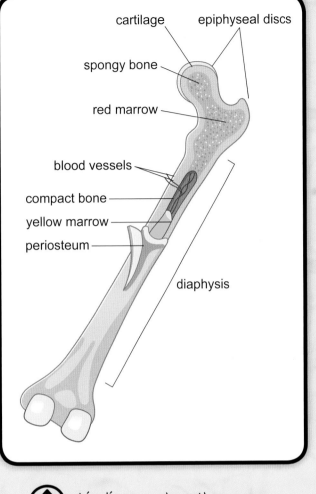

This diagram shows the internal structure of a bone.

The center of a bone is a light material called **spongy bone** (cancellous bone), arranged as a network of thin bars. These run in many different directions, forming a three-dimensional mesh. The large spaces between the bars may be filled with jelly-like material called bone marrow. Red bone marrow is found at the ends of long bones such as the femur (thighbone) and is involved in the production of red blood cells. Yellow bone marrow fills the spaces in the shafts of long bones and is mainly fat.

The internal structures of most bones are basically similar, but there are some differences. In some skull bones there is no spongy bone, just a series of air spaces (**sinuses**), and the flat bones of the cranium have two thin plates of compact bone, with spongy bone sandwiched between them. Irregular bones and short bones have varying amounts of spongy and compact bone.

Bone Marrow

Red bone marrow produces all the red blood cells and some of the white blood cells in the body. Yellow bone marrow is mainly made up of fat cells. When babies are born, all the bones contain red marrow. By the time children are six or seven years old, some of the red marrow becomes yellow marrow. This process continues, and in most adults red marrow is found only at the ends of the long bones, such as the femur; in flat bones, such as the ribs and sternum; and in the pelvic girdle.

This electron micrograph shows red and white blood cells in the bone marrow. The dark areas are normally occupied by blood vessels.

Blood cell production

Blood cells age and are broken down, so new ones have to be made continually to replace them. The red bone marrow contains special stem cells from which all the different types of blood cells can be made. The stem cells are like blank cells. As they grow and divide, they change and develop, becoming more and more specialized at each stage, until they eventually become new blood cells. Both white blood cells, which are involved in the body's **immune system**, and red blood cells, which transport oxygen around the body, are produced by bone marrow. Red blood cells only live for about 120 days. Healthy adults have about 250 million red blood cells in every drop of blood. To keep them at this concentration, the bone marrow has to produce at least two million new red blood cells every second!

Control of blood cell production

Blood cell production is controlled by a feedback loop. Red blood cells carry oxygen around the body. If there are too few red blood cells, the level of oxygen in the blood drops. The kidneys detect this and release a **hormone** called erythropoietin. This travels around the body in the blood, and when it reaches the bone marrow it speeds up the production of red blood cells. When the oxygen level gets back to normal, the kidneys stop releasing erythropoietin, and red blood cell production slows down again.

Bone marrow problems

There are a number of possible reasons why bone marrow may not produce blood cells properly:

- Some children are born with defective bone marrow.
- Chemicals, such as lead (found in water in buildings with old lead pipes and in the air in areas with high levels of air pollution), benzene (found in some dyes and fuels), and arsenic (a poisonous chemical sometimes used in pesticides), can damage bone marrow.
- X-rays and other types of radiation damage bone marrow.
- Some types of leukemia, a bone marrow disease, can clog up the bone marrow with malformed white blood cells.

A bone marrow transplant can help in some of these cases.

IN FOCUS: BONE MARROW TRANSPLANTS

A bone marrow transplant may be used to treat some bone marrow problems. Red bone marrow from a healthy donor is injected into the bloodstream of the patient. The stem cells travel around in the blood until they reach the patient's bone marrow. They settle there and begin to produce healthy blood cells. It is often difficult to find a suitable donor, so stem cells from other sources, such as donated umbilical cord blood, may be used for transplant in some patients.

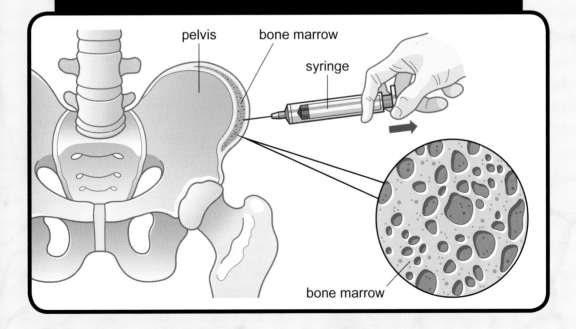

Bone marrow is removed from a donor's hip bone to be used in a bone marrow transplant to treat a patient.

Broken Bones

Bones are strong, but an accident such as an awkward fall can break them. The medical term for a broken bone is a "**fracture**." Some are simple and mend easily, while others are more complicated and may need surgery to help to repair them.

Type of fracture	What happens to the bone?
Greenstick fracture	This occurs in young children. Their bones are more flexible than adults' bones, so although one side of the bone may be broken, the other side may simply bend a little.
Partial fracture	The bone does not break completely into separate pieces. This is also called an incomplete fracture.
Stress	This may be a single crack or a mass of many tiny cracks in the bone, without any other damage.
Chip	A small piece of bone breaks off the main bone.
Simple fracture	The bone snaps into two pieces, but they stay in line with each other.
Compound fracture	This is like a simple fracture, but one or both of the broken ends of the bone stick out through the skin.
Comminuted fracture	The bone breaks into two, and part of it is shattered into smaller fragments.
Impacted fracture	The bone breaks into two pieces, and one is forced a little way inside the other.

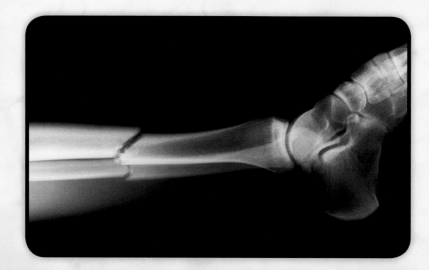

This X-ray shows a multiple fracture to the lower leg. Both the tibia and fibula have been broken.

HEALTH FOCUS: Sports-related fractures

The most common sports-related fracture is of the collarbone (**clavicle**). This can get damaged as the result of a clumsy fall. If you land on an arm stretched out to catch yourself as you fall, you can put huge pressure on the collarbone, snapping it in two.

Stress fractures, usually of the shinbones, are the result of an action being repeated over and over again, such as the thumping of feet on a hard track by runners and jumpers. Wearing running shoes with good support can help to prevent stress fractures.

Treating fractures

To prevent any further damage, broken bones need to be kept as still as possible. A sling can support a broken arm, and **splints** can keep a broken leg rigid. X-rays give accurate information about the fracture. If it is a simple fracture, wet plaster bandages are wrapped around the bone, drying and hardening to form a protective cast. Bones that have moved out of alignment need to be repositioned, and some complicated fractures may need surgery to insert metal pins for extra strength.

How bones heal

When a bone is broken, red blood cells pour out from the damaged blood vessels, forming a blood clot at the site of the break. Tiny blood vessels called capillaries slowly grow into the clot, and dead and damaged bone tissue is removed by white blood cells and osteoclasts. Strong fibers form, connecting the ends of the bone. Cartilage forms in between, and gradually osteoblasts make new spongy bone tissue. Compact bone then forms around the new spongy bone. This whole process may take several months.

The plaster cast and sling around this patient's arm will stop the broken bones from moving, allowing them to heal.

Bone Diseases

Although our bones are usually strong and healthy, there are various diseases that can affect them. Some are more serious than others. Different diseases affect people of different ages and have different causes, and therefore different treatments are required.

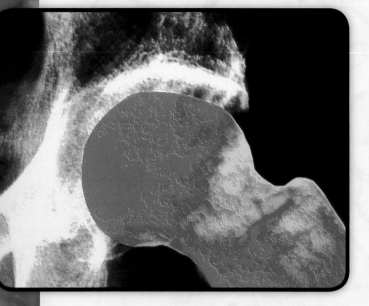

This color X-ray shows the upper part of the femur, affected by osteoporosis. The parts colored yellow-orange are fractures.

Osteoporosis

Osteoporosis is the weakening of bones as we age. The amount of minerals in our bones gradually decreases, and bone tissue is broken down more quickly than new tissue is made. The bars of the spongy bone become weakened, making the bones brittle and more likely to break easily. Fractures can occur just from normal activities—we may say older people fall and break a hip, but it would often be more accurate to say that the hip bone fractured and caused them to fall. Osteoporosis is a painful condition, also causing shrinkage and hunching of the backbone.

Osteoporosis causes more problems in women than in men, as the process of bone breakdown begins much earlier in women. In women, osteoporosis can start sometime after the age of 30 and accelerate in later middle age as hormone levels decrease. Hormones help to maintain bone strength. Since hormone levels remain at a higher level for longer in men than in women, osteoporosis does not usually begin in men until after the age of 60. Hormone replacement therapy (HRT) and calcium supplements can help to prevent osteoporosis. A diet rich in vitamins and minerals, particularly calcium and phosphorus, can reduce the risk of developing osteoporosis. Weight-bearing exercise, such as walking, also plays an important role by stimulating the production of more new bone tissue.

Osteomyelitis

Bones can be infected by **microorganisms** such as *Streptococcus aureus*. **Bacteria** can get into the bone from outside the body, when a bone is broken, or from a wound or surgery. They can also spread inside the body from other infected places, such as abscesses in the teeth. Infections in bones (osteomyelitis) cause fever, sweating, and sickness. There may be pus and swelling at the site of infection. Osteomyelitis is usually treated successfully with **antibiotics**.

Rickets and osteomalacia

Vitamin D is needed for calcium to be able to accumulate in bones as they grow. Without vitamin D, calcium does not accumulate, and the bones become soft and rubbery. This is called rickets, a disease in which children's bones are too weak to grow properly. The leg bones are not strong enough to carry the weight of the body, and so they are bent and bowed. Rickets is much less common in developed countries than it was in the past because diet and living conditions have greatly improved. In adults, lack of vitamin D prevents new bone tissue from being made, and the bones feel painful and tender. This is adult rickets, also called osteomalacia.

Bone tumors

Bones may have some lumps that do no harm at all, but **tumors** can also arise in bones. Although all bone tumors need to be investigated and treated, many are not **cancerous**. Osteosarcomas are the most common type of bone cancer, and, although they may affect older people, they usually occur in people between 10 and 20 years old. They can occur in any part of the body, but are usually found at the ends of the leg bones or ribs. The area may be painful, but often there are no symptoms and the disease may only be discovered when the bone breaks at the site of the tumor.

Osteosarcomas can be removed surgically, and then the patient usually receives chemotherapy (drug treatment) to kill any remaining tumor cells. Recent advances in treatment mean that these tumors can now often be completely cured.

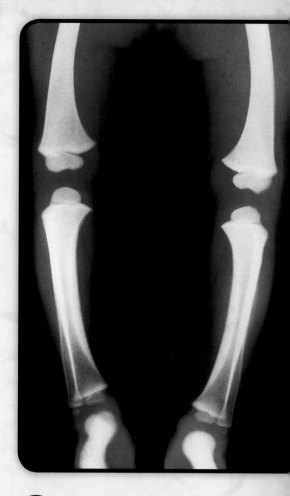

This X-ray shows the bending of the leg bones that is typical in a child suffering from rickets.

IN FOCUS: INHERITED DISEASES

Some children are born with "brittle bone disease" (*osteogenesis imperfecta*). The bones do not contain enough **proteins** and minerals, so they are very weak and snap easily. Some babies even have broken bones when they are born. These children need to be looked after very carefully and protected from any situations where the bones may be put under strain. This means babies are very limited in what they can do. However, as they grow older, with a suitable diet and treatment, the bones gradually get stronger, so these children are more able to lead a normal, active life.

Different Joints

Joints are the places where two bones meet. They allow the bones to move freely past each other, so that we can move all the parts of our bodies. Different types of joints allow different movements. There are two main types of joint in the human skeleton: hinge joints and ball-and-socket joints.

Hinge joints

Hinge joints work like the hinge of a door, allowing movement in one direction—you can move a door back and forth, but you cannot move it up and down or around and around. The elbow joint is a hinge joint: if you keep your upper arm completely still, you can move your lower arm up and down, but you cannot wiggle it from side to side or move it around in a circle. The knee is also a hinge joint.

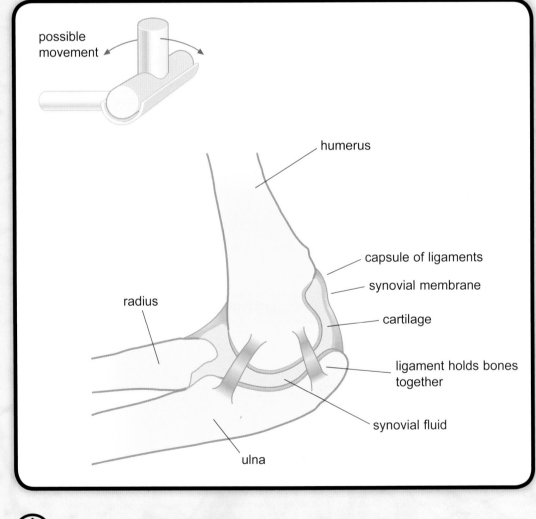

possible movement

humerus

capsule of ligaments

synovial membrane

cartilage

radius

ligament holds bones together

synovial fluid

ulna

The hinge joint of the elbow allows the lower arm to move up and down.

Ball-and-socket joints

Ball-and-socket joints allow a much wider range of movements than hinge joints. The end of one bone is a round lump (the ball) that fits snugly into a curved space (the socket) in the other bone. The shoulder joint, where the end of the humerus fits into the shoulder blade, is a ball-and-socket joint. Because of its design, you have a full range of movements—you can move your upper arm in just about any direction you want to.

The other major ball-and-socket joint is the hip joint, where the ball of the femur fits into the socket of the pelvic girdle. Although the bones could move very freely, tough bands of fibers limit their movements, so for most people the hip joint has a smaller range of movements than the shoulder joint.

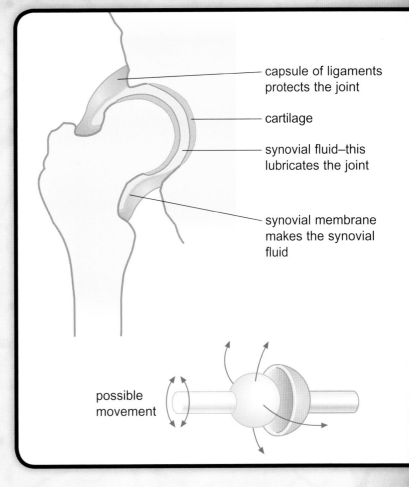

capsule of ligaments protects the joint

cartilage

synovial fluid—this lubricates the joint

synovial membrane makes the synovial fluid

possible movement

The ball-and-socket joint of the hip allows the leg to move freely in most directions.

IN FOCUS: OTHER JOINTS

Not all our joints follow these two designs. Other types of joint include:

- fixed joints, which are found between the bones of the skull. They are knitted tightly together and allow no movement.
- gliding joints of the wrist and ankle, which allow one bone to glide smoothly over the surface of another
- condyloid joints of the wrist and knuckles, which allow movement up and down, and from side to side
- saddle joints between the thumb bone and the wrist bones, which allow the thumb to move in all directions
- pivot joints, which allow a rotating movement of one bone around part of another. This type of joint in the neck allows us to turn our head from side to side: the top, ring-shaped vertebra balances on a point of the vertebra below it.

Inside Joints

Even the smallest joints are complex constructions. Structures are needed to keep the bones in place, to prevent the ends of the bones from being damaged, and to ensure that movements are smooth.

Fixed joints

In some fixed joints, bones are knitted together tightly by strong fibers, preventing movement. These are found between the bones of the skull.

Joints can also be held tightly together by pieces of cartilage. These can be found at the joint between the first rib and the sternum, and also where bones join at the front of the pelvic girdle.

Moving joints

Joints that allow bone movement have a more complex structure than fixed joints and are called synovial joints. The ends of each bone are covered with a layer of smooth cartilage, to reduce friction between them as they move past each other. The cartilage also acts as a cushion, absorbing shock.

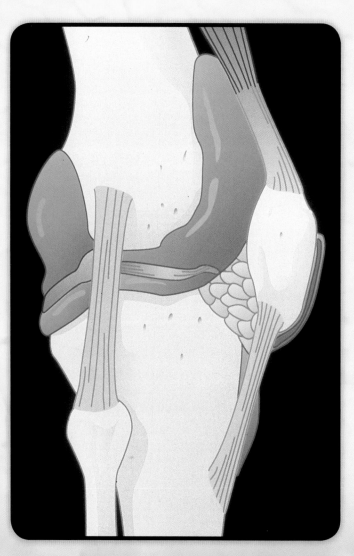

This diagram shows the structures inside a synovial joint—in this case, the knee joint. You can see how the space between the bones is filled with synovial fluid (blue).

The whole joint is surrounded by the articular capsule, a sleeve-like cover that links the bones together. The outer layer of the capsule is made of tough fibers, which are flexible enough to allow movement, but difficult to stretch, in order to prevent the bones from moving out of position. The inner layer, the synovial membrane, makes a liquid called synovial fluid. This fluid fills the space between the bones, the synovial cavity, and lubricates the inside surfaces of the joint.

Ligaments

Ligaments are tough bands of fiber that hold the joint together. They are really part of the articular capsule and are very strong, to prevent the joint from being strained. Some ligaments are tiny, but some are much larger and have their own names. The hip joint has to take the full weight of the body, so the ligaments that hold the ball of the femur in the socket of the pelvis are extremely strong.

Extra structures

In addition to the major structures of synovial joints, some contain additional structures. Extra bands called accessory ligaments can help to hold a joint together and are important in the knee joint. Some joints have small, fluid-filled sacs or pads called **bursae** that act as a cushion when the skin, a tendon, or a muscle may rub over a bone.

Some synovial membranes contain fat pads, as in the knee joint. Discs of cartilage may lie between the bones, attached to the articular capsule, and help to maintain the stability of the joint.

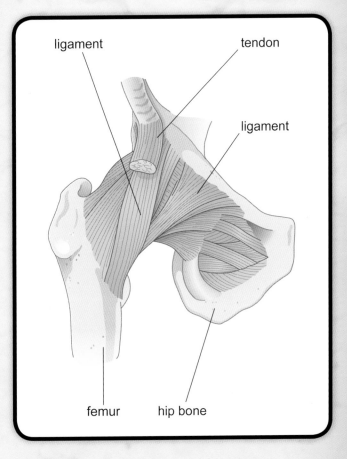

This diagram shows some of the ligaments that hold the hip joint together.

HEALTH FOCUS: Warming up

When a joint is immobile for a while, the synovial fluid becomes thicker and jelly-like. A gentle warm-up before doing any vigorous exercise stimulates the production and release of synovial fluid. As the joint begins to move, the fluid becomes runnier. Warming up reduces the risk of joint injuries.

Joints are complicated structures, allowing us to move our bodies in many different ways. They are designed to be strong and stand up to normal wear and tear. However, moving bones too far, too fast, or in the wrong direction can damage the joints and cause a variety of injuries.

Sprain

Sprains are common injuries, caused by twisting a joint too far. When the ligaments are overstressed, they become stretched or even torn. The joint may swell, and a bruise may develop as blood leaks out of damaged blood vessels around the injury. Sprains can be very painful, but treatment with an ice pack can help to reduce swelling. Sprains usually heal well if the joint is rested and not put under further stress for a while.

You are more likely to sprain an ankle than any other joint. Most people walk and run often, and it is easy to lose your footing or trip on uneven ground, twisting the ankle and spraining it.

This doctor and athlete are looking at an X-ray of the athlete's knee injury and discussing possible treatments.

HEALTH FOCUS: RICE treatment

"RICE" is a way of remembering a good way of treating non-serious injuries, such as minor sprains or strains. RICE stands for:

R = rest (to avoid making the injury worse)
I = ice (keeping the injured joint cold can reduce pain)
C = compression (wrapping the joint can reduce swelling)
E = elevation (prevents fluid from accumulating, which makes the joint swell)

For more serious injuries, or if you are in any doubt, you should seek medical help.

HEALTH FOCUS: Joint injuries and sports

Injuries to joints can prevent sports activities for a while. No matter how frustrating it may be, it makes sense to follow the doctor's advice and not start training again too soon, in order to give the joint time to heal properly. Stretched and torn ligaments take time to heal, dislocated bones need time to settle back into place and for any damaged tissue to heal, and inflammation takes time to subside. If you are impatient and use the joint again too soon, you risk aggravating the injury and needing even more time away from training.

Dislocation

Dislocation occurs when the two bones of a joint become separated. The joint that is most commonly dislocated is the shoulder, as the head of the humerus moves out of the socket of the shoulder blade. Usually the humerus moves in front of the shoulder blade, rather than behind it.

This injury can be the result of an awkward fall, often in a physical sport such as football. Skilled doctors or nurses can manipulate the joint and push the humerus back into its correct position. An X-ray may be taken to make sure that there are no fractures. After dislocation, it is very important to rest the joint in order to give it a chance to heal fully.

Inflammation

Repeated, vigorous movements can lead to **inflammation** of the bursae inside a joint. The joint can become swollen as fluid collects inside it, and movement may be painful and limited. Injuries of this sort were often given names that reflected the type of activity that caused them— for example, "housemaid's knee" as the result of kneeling for long periods, and "tennis elbow" as the result of overusing the elbow joint.

Injuries like this will heal naturally if the joint is rested. An ice pack can help the inflammation to subside, and anti-inflammatory injections may also help. The extra fluid will slowly drain away, and the swelling will go down so that movement is possible again.

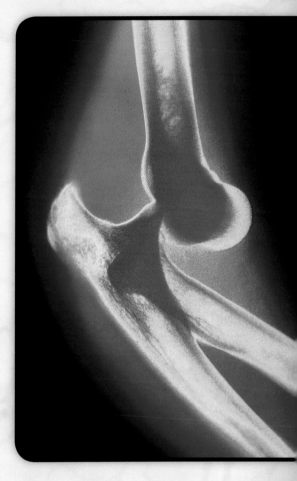

This diagram shows what happens when an elbow joint is dislocated.

Knee Injuries

The knee joint is the largest and most complex joint in the body. It is designed to allow the leg to bend, but it also needs to be rigid enough to hold the body stable when we stand still. It can be injured in a variety of ways, and damage can involve the bones themselves, the ligaments, cartilage, and tendons of muscles.

The knee joint

Three bones meet at the knee joint: the femur, **tibia**, and patella. Ligaments also link the **fibula** to the knee joint. The end of each bone is covered with a protective layer of cartilage. Pads of cartilage lie between the bones, acting as shock absorbers. Several bursae also cushion the knee joint.

Four strong ligaments bind the bones together:

- Two cruciate ligaments make an X-shape as they cross over each other.
- Two collateral ligaments run down the sides of the knee joint.

The patella is held in place in front of the end of the femur.

Torn cartilage

The pads of cartilage inside the joint may be damaged if the knee receives a direct blow or is twisted awkwardly. If cartilage becomes wedged between the bones, the joint may "lock" and cause a lot of pain. Doctors may remove small pieces of cartilage that have broken off the main cartilage or, if the cartilage is badly damaged, remove it entirely. Recently, research has shown that stem cells can be used to rebuild damaged cartilage in the knee.

Torn ligaments

Ligaments may be torn by sudden twisting or by a direct blow, as in a football tackle. The person may hear a "popping" sound, and the leg may buckle under his or her weight.

IN FOCUS: INSIDE KNEES

Until recent years, doctors had no easy way of finding out the extent of damage that may have occurred inside a knee joint. In the 1970s, Japanese surgeons developed the arthroscope, a small, illuminated tube that can be inserted into the knee through a small cut. This provides a clear view of the inside of the knee, sending detailed pictures to a monitor. Doctors can also now use microsurgical operating techniques, often needing a cut less than 1 centimeter (0.4 inch) long and requiring just a single stitch! This means that the recovery time from knee operations is much, much shorter than it used to be.

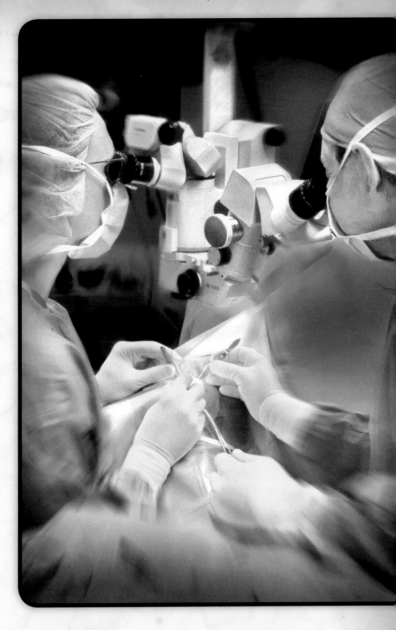

This picture shows surgeons operating on a patient's knee using microsurgery.

If the ligament is damaged but not completely torn, a protective brace may be worn and exercises can be prescribed to strengthen the surrounding muscles.

If the ligament is completely torn, it can be repaired surgically. Collateral ligaments can be re-attached to the bones. Cruciate ligaments can be attached to sutures (strong threads) that are then threaded through specially drilled holes in the femur, with the ends tied to hold them in place. Doctors may also use pieces of ligament from elsewhere in the body to help them repair these ligaments. Research is being conducted to try to find the best material to make artificial ligaments; several have been tried, including Gore-Tex, Dacron, and carbon fiber, but with very limited success.

HEALTH FOCUS: "Runner's knee"

"Runner's knee" is one of the most common knee problems for runners, especially those who run long distances or on hills. It may be caused by always walking or running on the same side of the road. Roads slope down a little at the sides, so unless you change sides, one knee is constantly stretched more than the other. In normal movement, the patella slides back and forth. In "runner's knee" it moves sideways a little as well, causing aching and tenderness underneath the patella. The pain usually gets worse when the person walks down stairs or squats down. Rest, and use of a brace to keep the patella central, may help to relieve the condition.

Arthritis

"Arthritis" is the name given to painful, swollen joints. It can have many different causes, but in most cases arthritis falls into one of two main types.

Osteoarthritis

Osteoarthritis is caused by the cartilage at the end of the joints wearing away. When you move your joints, the cartilage at the end of the bones is worn. Normally, the body replaces the cartilage, but sometimes it is worn away more quickly than the body can replace it. Eventually the bone surfaces become exposed and the joint becomes very painful. Large weight-bearing joints like the hip and knee are particularly likely to be affected.

Rheumatoid arthritis

While osteoarthritis is a result of wear on the joints, the causes of rheumatoid arthritis are more complex. It is probably caused by an autoimmune response. This means that the body's immune system, instead of attacking germs from outside the body, attacks its own tissue, in this case the synovial membrane in the body's joints. The cartilage becomes very soft and wears away quickly in many joints at the same time.

Who is affected?

Many people believe that only older people are affected by arthritis, but this is not strictly true. Osteoarthritis does seem to be a natural product of the aging process, but there are other causes, too. Research has suggested that arthritis may be linked to certain **genes**, meaning that some people are born with a higher risk of suffering from arthritis than others.

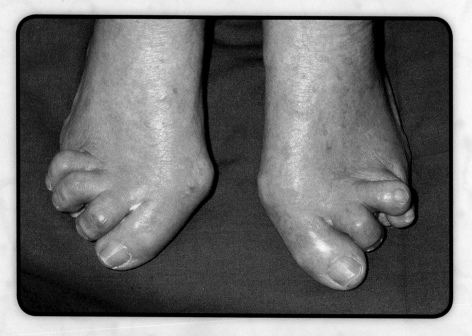

 This photograph shows severe damage caused by arthritis. Standing and walking must be very painful for this person.

Rheumatoid arthritis, on the other hand, normally starts to show itself between the ages of 20 and 50, with women more likely to be affected than men. There is even a form of rheumatoid arthritis that appears in very young children between the ages of two and five.

Dealing with arthritis

In most cases, treatment of arthritis is done by relieving the symptoms—for example, through anti-inflammatory drugs that reduce the inflammation inside the joints. Medication is normally part of a three-step treatment that includes rest, to allow joints to reduce inflammation, and exercise, to rebuild strength in the joint. **Occupational therapists** can also help people to find easier ways of doing normal activities, avoiding the use of painful joints. In extreme cases of arthritis, doctors can sometimes replace the affected joints.

Gold cure?

In the early part of the 20th century, scientists discovered that compounds of gold, whether swallowed or injected, could block the immune system and therefore be an effective treatment for rheumatoid arthritis. However, this treatment has harmful side effects, affecting the kidneys, and is now used with great caution.

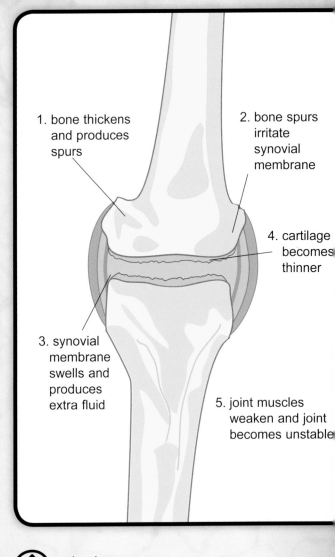

1. bone thickens and produces spurs

2. bone spurs irritate synovial membrane

4. cartilage becomes thinner

3. synovial membrane swells and produces extra fluid

5. joint muscles weaken and joint becomes unstable

⬆ This diagram shows how osteoarthritis affects a knee joint.

HEALTH FOCUS: Arthritis and sports

Osteoarthritis can affect younger people, especially if joints are overexercised. There are cases of professional athletes who have suffered from the condition because they have continued to play when injured. Anesthetic sprays and creams prevent messages from traveling from sensory receptors to the brain. This takes away the immediate pain of an injury, so the person can continue to play, but the injury itself may actually be getting worse and worse. The overuse of **steroids**, to help with joint pain, has also been linked to the development of arthritis at a young age.

Joint Replacements

Modern advances in medicine allow doctors to replace some damaged and worn-out joints with artificial ones. This gives patients freedom from pain and allows them to live more active lives than they would otherwise be able to enjoy.

Damaged joints

The most common reason for replacement of a joint is osteoarthritis. The cartilage covering the ends of the bones wears away, causing pain when the joint is moved as the bones rub against each other. Knees and hips are the most common joints to be replaced with artificial ones. Other joints, such as shoulders, ankles, wrists, and knuckles, can also be replaced.

This picture shows an artificial hip joint. The long shaft is inserted into a hole in the femur, and the socket is attached to the pelvis.

IN FOCUS: THE FIRST ARTIFICIAL HIP JOINT

Doctors have tried for many years to find a way of replacing damaged and worn-out joints. Some of the first experiments were carried out in the 18th century by German doctors using ivory, but these were not successful. In the 20th century, more attempts were made, and eventually a breakthrough was made in the late 1960s by a British **orthopedic** surgeon, Sir John Charnley. He designed and used a metal ball and a plastic socket for a new hip joint, cementing the pieces in place with a plastic cement that was usually used by dentists. After his pioneering work, many other surgeons refined and perfected the techniques. Now around 300,000 knee replacements and 200,000 hip replacements are carried out each year in the United States alone.

New developments

Alongside the developments in surgical techniques used in joint replacement have been developments in the materials used for the replacement parts. Some surgeons now use the metal titanium for parts of the new joints. Titanium is more flexible and can support even greater loads than the natural bone. Another new development is an artificial knee joint covered with beads of cobalt. These beads encourage new bone material to grow over the joint, making it stronger and more permanent than just using cement. Other materials that may be useful in artificial joints, such as highly crosslinked polyethylene, are being given trials.

Replacing a hip joint

There are two parts to the operation to replace a hip joint: attaching the new "ball" to the femur, and replacing the socket of the pelvic girdle. Doctors first dislocate the hip so that they can work on the joint. The top of the femur is removed and the socket in the pelvis is carved out until it is exactly the right shape to hold the new shell. Once the shape is right, the shell may be held in place by the tightness of the fit, by screws, or by special cement. A hole is then drilled into the femur, and the shaft that holds the new ball is inserted. This can also be held by fitting screws or cement. The metal ball is attached to the shaft and the joint is reassembled.

After an operation

Patients are usually encouraged to start moving around again soon after a joint replacement. Doctors may use a CPM (constant passive motion) device after a knee replacement. This motorized apparatus moves the joint continuously, even while the patient is asleep, without requiring any effort from the patient. Use of CPM can speed up the healing process considerably.

The full range of movement may not be possible with a replacement joint, but there is usually more movement and less pain than with a severely arthritic joint. Patients are advised to continue with as many normal everyday activities as they can, but to avoid vigorous sports such as tennis and jogging.

Most replacement hips, knees, and shoulders last for 10 to 15 years. Gradually, the parts wear loose in the bones, and this causes pain as the person moves. Another operation is then needed—either to insert another replacement joint, or to make the existing joint fit more tightly into the bone.

This X-ray shows the leg bones with an artificial knee joint in place.

Spine

The spine, or vertebral column, provides an upright support for the upper body. It is made up of a stack of small bones, the vertebrae, piled one on top of another. The bony canal that runs through the vertebrae provides a protective tube for the nerves of the spinal cord.

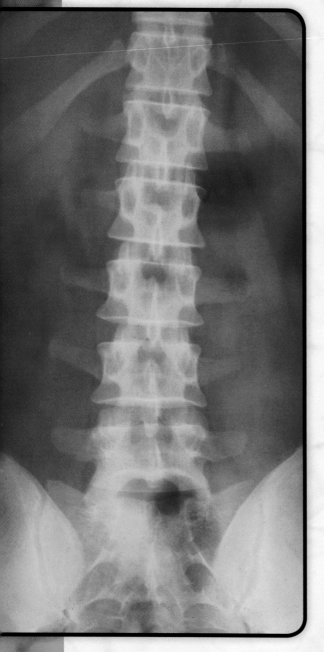

This X-ray shows some of the vertebrae that make up the spine.

The vertebral column contains 33 vertebrae, some of which are fused together. Each vertebra is slightly different in shape from the ones above and below, so they fit together to make a flexible column that allows us to bend back and forth and twist from side to side. When we stand normally, the spine curves gently in and out, to absorb shock, increase its strength, and ensure that the body weight is evenly distributed.

The vertebral column

The vertebrae can be thought of in groups:

- **Cervical**: The top seven vertebrae make up the neck. The first vertebra (the atlas) supports the head, and the joint between the atlas and the skull allows the head to nod up and down. The pivot joint between the atlas and the second vertebra (the axis) allows the head to turn from side to side.
- **Thoracic**: The next 12 vertebrae form the back of the chest. These increase in size as they go downward. Each thoracic vertebra is attached to a pair of ribs.
- **Lumbar**: The five lumbar vertebrae are the biggest and strongest. They lie between the chest and the pelvic girdle, and they support the powerful muscles of the lower back.
- **Sacral**: The five sacral vertebrae are separate in children but gradually fuse together between the ages of 16 and 30 to make one strong, curved bone—the **sacrum**. This adds strength to the pelvic girdle and helps to keep it stable.
- **Coccyx**: The last three, four, or five vertebrae also fuse together to make the coccyx, a tiny tailbone at the base of the spine.

What is a vertebra like?

Although each vertebra is different, they all follow the same basic design. The "body" is the solid front (ventral) part of a vertebra. It faces inward, and it is this part that carries the weight of the rest of the body.

Seven pieces of bone, called processes, jut out of the back (dorsal) and sides of the vertebral body. The two transverse processes are the sites where muscles are attached. The five articular processes link directly to the vertebrae above and below, stopping the vertebra from slipping out of position.

Together, these pieces form a bony ring, with the body of the vertebra at the front and the other pieces of bone arranged into the vertebral arch.

Protecting nerves

When the vertebrae, held together by ligaments, are stacked one on top of the other, the individual bony rings line up to make a hollow column. The spinal cord is a bundle of nerves running through this channel from the base of the vertebral column to the brain. Nerves run from the body, in between the vertebrae, and connect with the spinal cord. The spinal cord is very important, carrying messages to and from the brain and every part of the body. Damage to the spinal cord can result in **paralysis** and loss of function, and so the protection offered by the bony column of the spine is extremely important.

Discs

Between each of the vertebrae is a disc of cartilage. The discs act as cushions to absorb shock. They also allow movement and protect the bones by stopping the vertebrae from rubbing together.

This picture shows the structure of one vertebra. You can see the space through which the spinal cord passes.

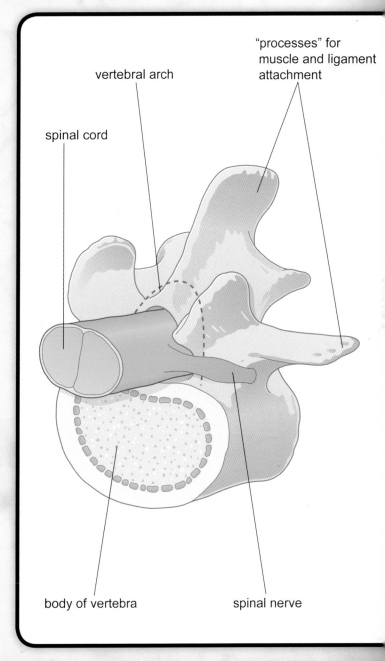

"processes" for muscle and ligament attachment

vertebral arch

spinal cord

body of vertebra

spinal nerve

Taking Care of Your Spine

Our spine allows us to carry out a wide range of activities, yet people may be damaging their spines through many of the things they do every day. The information on this page may help you to take care of your spine.

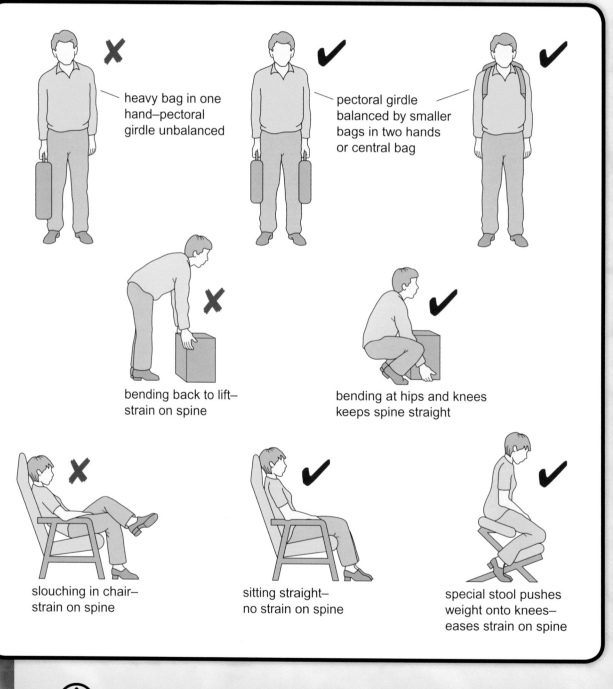

heavy bag in one hand—pectoral girdle unbalanced

pectoral girdle balanced by smaller bags in two hands or central bag

bending back to lift—strain on spine

bending at hips and knees keeps spine straight

slouching in chair—strain on spine

sitting straight—no strain on spine

special stool pushes weight onto knees—eases strain on spine

These diagrams show some ways in which you can take care of your spine.

Carrying

The natural curves of the spine balance the body evenly, keeping the hips and shoulders more or less horizontal and making sure the weight is evenly distributed.

Carrying a heavy bag on one shoulder, or in one hand, can completely distort this balance. The weight pulls down on one side, and the other side rises to compensate.

You can prevent this, yet still carry the same weight, either by sharing the load between two smaller bags, one for each hand, or by carrying it all in one central bag like a backpack. The backpack must be worn correctly, with a strap over each shoulder, to distribute the weight evenly over both shoulders.

Bending and lifting

If you curve your spine to reach down to pick up an object, you put a tremendous strain on it. A much better way is to bend your hips and knees and pick the object up with your spine as straight as possible, minimizing the strain on it.

Posture

We all lounge lazily in a chair sometimes, but this puts quite a strain on your lumbar vertebra. It really is not a good idea to sit like this regularly or for long periods. Try to sit far back into your chair, with your spine as vertical as possible, so you are sitting on your bottom and not on your lower spine.

Hunching over a desk can make your shoulders ache—and it is not good for your spine. Try to sit with your back straight. Some office chairs are designed to take the strain off the back by spreading some strain to your knees.

HEALTH FOCUS: Sports and spines

Some sports demand a lot more of the spine than others. Weight lifters usually wear a strong belt to provide extra support for their lumbar vertebrae. This saves them a lot of damage to the spine.

Warming up before you begin an activity is just as important for your spine as it is for other muscles and bones. Slow, gentle stretching movements can help to prevent strains and other injuries.

Spinal Problems and Injuries

The spine is such a complex set of bones, bearing the whole weight of the body, that it is hardly surprising that injuries occur. Some are bone problems, but many backaches are due mainly to muscular strain and do not directly involve any bones.

Slipped disc

Between each vertebra is a disc of cartilage that acts as a shock absorber and cushion. Normally, the weight of the body pulls down evenly, pressing on the discs evenly. If the weight is uneven, as in carrying a heavy weight on one side or bending a long way to one side, the discs will be pressed unevenly. Part of a disc may jut out past the vertebral column; this is known as a "slipped" disc. If this presses on one of the spinal nerves, it can be extremely painful.

The treatment for a slipped disc depends on the extent of the injury. It may be enough simply to rest in bed, or gentle exercise and heat treatment may help. Traction—using a system of weights and pulleys—may be used to exert pulling forces on the spine to alleviate the problem. If the disc is badly damaged, an operation may be necessary to remove it completely and fuse the vertebrae together.

Broken back

The real danger of a "broken back," or "broken neck," is damage to the spinal cord. There are two main types of spinal fracture.

This man is wearing a neck brace to support his neck while he recovers from a spine injury.

- Compression fractures occur when the body of one or more vertebrae is crushed. If the damage is limited to the body, and the vertebral arch is intact, the spinal cord will probably not be damaged.
- Extension fractures occur when the spine is pulled and stretched. An example of this is a severe whiplash injury that may be sustained in a car crash, or a horse-riding fall. The neck is forced backward, the atlas vertebra breaks, and part of the axis may even be snapped. A great force can separate the skull and these two vertebrae from the rest of the spine and may break the spinal cord.

If the spinal cord is not damaged, support may be given with a neck collar or brace. If the spinal cord is damaged, the signals along nerves to and from the brain will be interrupted, which may result in varying degrees of paralysis that will require long-term treatment and care.

Unusual curves

A normal spine is gently curved, but some people suffer from slightly different spinal curves.

The most common is a scoliosis, in which the spine curves from one side to the other, giving a twisted appearance. Much rarer is a kyphosis, in which the thoracic vertebrae are more curved than usual, giving a humped back. Lordosis, in which the lumbar region curves forward more than usual, is also uncommon.

Some babies may be born with these curvatures; in some people they may develop as part of the aging process, poor posture, or obesity; and in others these curvatures may be caused by diseases such as tuberculosis (which leads to degeneration of the vertebrae) or rickets (in which the bones do not form properly).

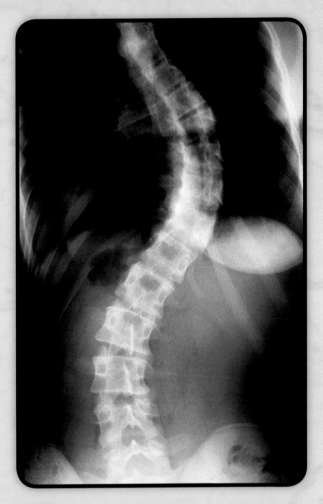

This X-ray shows the curvature of a spine affected by scoliosis.

IN FOCUS: SPINA BIFIDA

During the months before birth, the vertebral arches are open, but they gradually close around the spinal cord, enclosing it completely. In babies with spina bifida, the vertebral arches do not all close completely, so that the baby is born with part of the spinal cord jutting out through the skin, covered with just a thin membrane. This means that the spinal cord, the very important bundle of nerves that is usually protected by the spine, could easily be damaged or infected. In some babies with spina bifida, surgery may be carried out to close the gap. In others, healing may occur naturally during the first few months of life. However, many babies born with spina bifida do not survive very long. There is evidence to suggest that a mother taking folic acid supplements during early pregnancy significantly reduces the risk of her baby having spina bifida. In some countries, folic acid is added to foods, such as pasta, cereal, and bread, during the production process, to increase the amount people eat every day.

Skull

The 22 bones of the skull form a bony shell that protects the brain, eyes, and ears. They are all fixed together except for the lower jawbone, which is held in place by strong muscles. The skull bones are usually thought of in two sets: the cranial bones that make up the rounded, hollow part of the head, and the facial bones that make up the face.

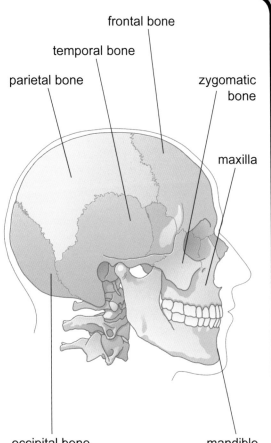

frontal bone

temporal bone

parietal bone

zygomatic bone

maxilla

occipital bone

mandible

This picture shows how the cranial and facial bones fit together.

Cranial bones

There are eight cranial bones, all joined together like a complicated jigsaw puzzle. The zigzag shapes of some of the bones means that they fit very tightly together. The joints between them, called sutures, are fixed joints, knitted together by strong fibers. Small, irregular sutural bones may occur between the sutures.

The cranial bones are:
- frontal bone—its domed shape makes the shell of the forehead and the tops of the eye sockets
- two parietal bones—form the top of the head and the sides above the ears
- occipital bone—forms the lower back part of the cranium
- two temporal bones—at each side, behind the ears
- sphenoid bone—shaped like a bat with its wings stretched out, this bone lies in front of the ears and stretches across the inside of the head from one side to the other; it helps to hold all the other cranial bones together
- ethmoid bone—forms the roof of the nasal cavity and other internal parts of the head.

Facial bones

There are 14 irregular facial bones. The picture shows how they all fit together to make the complex shape of the face.

The most obvious bones are the zygomatic bones (cheekbones), the nasal bones that form the bridge of the nose, and the maxillae (upper jawbones).

The lower mandible (jawbone) is the largest and strongest facial bone. It forms a loose hinge with part of the temporal bones and can move up and down, from side to side, and back and forth.

Sinuses

Some of the cranial and facial bones close to the nasal cavity have hollow spaces inside them called sinuses. These are lined with a mucus-producing membrane and drain into the nasal cavity. They act as resonating spaces, amplifying sounds when we talk and sing. Inflammation, usually due to an infection or an allergic reaction, is called sinusitis. It can cause a buildup of pressure inside the sinuses and lead to a bad headache.

Fontanelles

The skeleton of a newborn baby is soft and delicate. Gradually minerals are laid down and the bones harden and become stronger. At birth, there are small spaces between the cranial bones, just covered by membranes and skin, that allow the skull to change its size and shape during birth. They will eventually be the sites of the suture joints, but until the bones harden and fuse they are very vulnerable. They are called "soft spots," or fontanelles.

HEALTH FOCUS: Cleft palate and cleft lip

Usually, the maxillary bones that form the upper jaw of the face join before a baby is born. Sometimes, though, they are not properly joined at birth. The baby has a cleft palate or a cleft lip that may affect speech and swallowing. A cleft lip is usually closed surgically just a few weeks after birth. A cleft palate is usually closed between the ages of 12 and 18 months, before the baby starts to talk. **Speech therapy** may be needed, but the results are usually very good.

The baby in this photograph has a cleft lip.

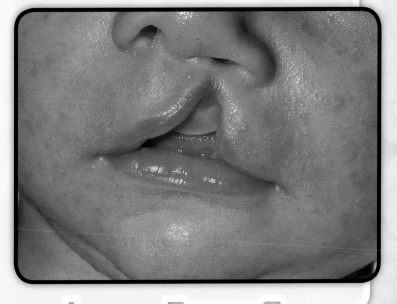

Ribcage

The ribcage is made up of the ribs, the sternum (breastbone), and the thoracic vertebrae. It forms a bony cage, enclosing and protecting the heart and lungs. Its flexibility allows the chest to expand and contract as we breathe in and out.

Sternum

The sternum is a flat, dagger-shaped bone about 15 centimeters (6 inches) long and 4 centimeters (1.5 inches) wide. It forms the center of the chest and provides anchorage for the ribs. It has three sections:

- a squarish upper section, with a notch on each side for the clavicles (collarbones) to attach to; the top pair of ribs is attached to this section, and the second pair is attached at the point where this section meets the middle section
- a long middle section, to which the rest of the ribs are attached
- a small, pointed lower section that does not change from cartilage into hardened bone until the age of about 40; it provides anchorage for some major muscles.

Ribs

Most people have 12 pairs of ribs. Each rib is a flat bone, curved and slightly twisted into a flattened half-circle shape. Each rib is linked at a joint to a thoracic vertebra at the back. The top seven pairs are joined to the sternum by strips of cartilage. The next three pairs are linked together by strips of cartilage, and this joins the cartilage of the seventh pair to link on to the sternum. The last two pairs are called "floating ribs"—they are not anchored to the sternum at all.

The ribcage encloses and protects the heart and lungs.

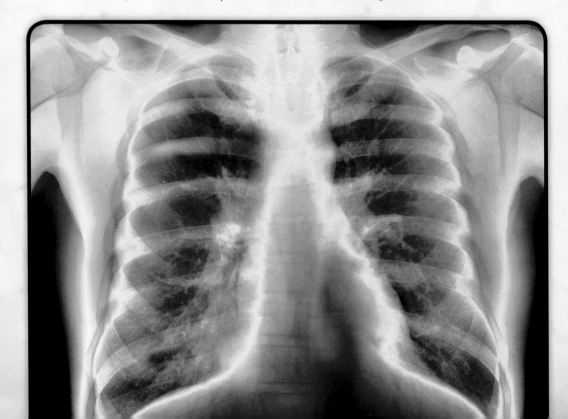

Each rib is linked to the ones above and below it by muscles that lie in the **intercostal** spaces between them. When these muscles contract, the ribs are moved upward and outward, expanding the chest space so that we can breathe in. When these muscles relax, the ribs move inward and downward, the chest space contracts, and we breathe out.

Broken ribs

A broken rib is the most common chest injury. It is usually the result of falling heavily; a direct blow, such as being thrust against the steering wheel in a car accident; or being crushed, such as a horse landing on its rider.

The ribs tend to break at the point where the greatest force is applied—in other words, where the chest was hit. They may also break at their weakest point, which is at the middle of the half circle shape where they are most curved.

Broken ribs may be very painful, but are not in themselves dangerous. However, they can lead to more serious injury if one of the fractured pieces damages internal organs such as the heart, lungs, liver, or **spleen**.

In many cases, cracked and broken ribs may be left to heal by themselves, possibly with bandages wrapped around the chest to prevent more damage. In more serious cases, an operation may be necessary.

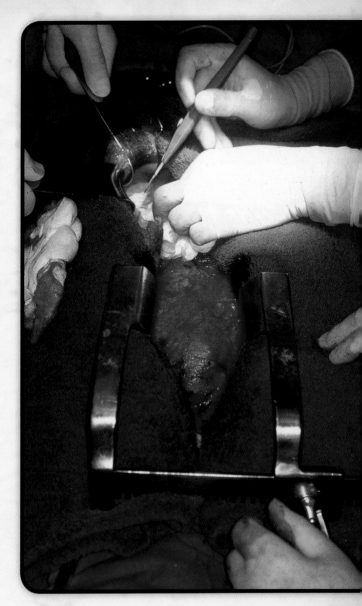

↑ In order to perform chest surgery, such as a heart transplant, doctors must use a metal retractor to keep the ribs apart.

IN FOCUS: CHEST SURGERY

If a patient needs a chest operation, such as heart surgery, doctors have to find a way to get inside the ribcage. They may do this by using a special clamp called a retractor to hold the ribs apart, and then they enter through the side of the ribcage. Alternatively, they may split the sternum down the middle to open the ribcage from above. The sternum can be stitched or stapled back together after the operation.

Arm and Hand

Our shoulder blades and collarbones form a horizontal crossbar to which our arms are attached. The shoulder joint allows the upper arm to move freely in any direction. We are able to use our arms and hands to do a wide variety of different things, such as picking up heavy objects, throwing things, holding on to things, and making tiny, precise movements.

Pectoral girdle

The scapulae (shoulder blades) and clavicles (collarbones) together form the **pectoral girdle**. The clavicles are joined one to each side of the sternum. The shoulder blades do not join on to each other or on to the vertebrae. Instead, they are held in place by a complex arrangement of powerful muscles and ligaments.

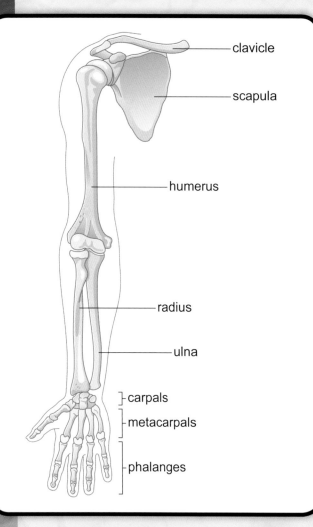

clavicle

scapula

humerus

radius

ulna

carpals

metacarpals

phalanges

↑ This diagram shows the bones that make up the part of the pectoral girdle, arm, and hand.

Upper arm

The upper arm consists of a single bone, the humerus, that moves freely in the ball-and-socket joint with the scapula. The shaft of the humerus is roughly cylindrical, widening at the bottom into a broad, flattened triangular shape to form the top part of the elbow joint.

Elbow joint

The elbow joint is a simple hinge joint, where the humerus meets the bones of the lower arm. It allows us to bend and straighten the arm. Overuse of this joint can result in swelling and tenderness, a condition known as "tennis elbow."

Lower arm

There are two bones in the lower arm: the **radius** and the **ulna**. The ulna is larger than the radius and runs from the elbow to the outside of the wrist. The smaller radius runs from the elbow to the thumb side of the wrist. The radius and ulna meet at pivot joints at the elbow and wrist.

The radius and ulna are connected by strong fibers that lie in the space between them. These fibers allow the two bones to roll over each other so that we can turn our hands over from palm down to palm up and back again.

Wrist

There are eight small bones, the carpals, in each wrist, arranged in two rows of four bones each, joined together by ligaments. The gliding joints allow the bones to slide smoothly over each other, giving the wrist its suppleness.

Hand

The flat part of the hand is made up of five long, thin bones, the **metacarpals**. These are linked directly to the finger bones, the **phalanges**. Each finger has three phalanges, but the thumb has only two.

We can move each finger bone up and down, bending our fingers. The special saddle joint between the first bone of the thumb and the metacarpal allows us to move the thumb in every direction.

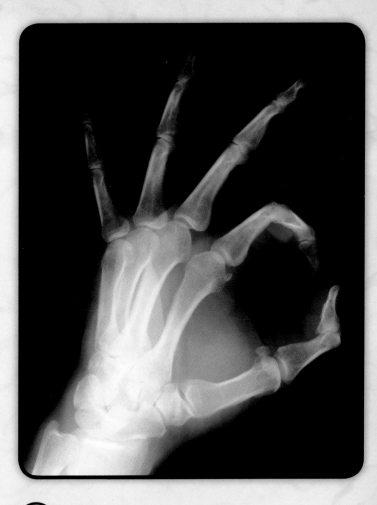

This X-ray shows the bones of the finger and thumb forming an "O." These bones allow us to carry out tiny, precise movements and are unique to humans and some other primates.

HEALTH FOCUS: Carpal tunnel syndrome

The carpal bones, together with fibrous tissue (ligaments), make a channel called the "carpal tunnel" through which a bundle of long tendons and nerves run. If this becomes inflamed, the nerves can get squeezed, causing pain and tingling, and making it hard to carry out small, delicate movements. This is carpal tunnel syndrome, and it is most common in people who use their fingers a lot—for example, people who do data entry on computers. Treatment is usually by rest and anti-inflammatory drugs. Sometimes an operation may be necessary to cut the ligament and ease the pressure.

Leg and Foot

The structure of the leg and foot is similar to that of the arm and hand. The pelvic girdle provides a horizontal crossbar to which the legs are attached at the hip joints. The bones of the legs are very strong, since they have to carry the weight of the whole body. The feet are flexible, allowing us to walk, run, and jump.

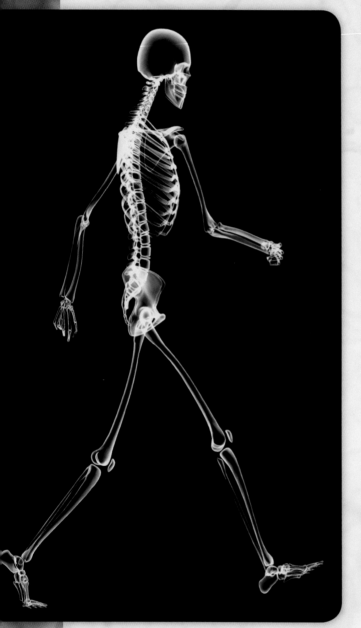

Pelvic girdle

The pelvic girdle is made up from the hip bones, the sacrum, and the coccyx. The hip bones are the broadest bones in the body and are made up from three smaller bones: the ilium, ischium, and pubis, which fuse together between the ages of 15 and 18. The pelvis provides attachment sites for large muscles and for the legs and allows the transfer of weight between the legs and spine. It also supports and protects organs in the lower abdomen.

There are important differences between the pelvic girdles of men and women. A man's pelvis is larger than that of a woman and is rounder. A woman's pelvis is wider and shallower, allowing a baby to pass through when it is born. These differences are valuable in helping archaeologists determine the sex of ancient skeletons.

Thigh

The thigh has a single bone, the femur. This is the heaviest, longest, and strongest bone in the human body. It is usually roughly one-quarter of the full height of an adult. It is attached to the pelvis by the ball-and-socket joint at the hip. The joint allows movement in all directions, but the extent of movement is strictly limited by very strong ligaments to prevent dislocation.

When we walk, muscles pull the bones in a carefully coordinated sequence.

Knee joint

The thigh and lower leg join at the knee. It is a hinge joint that allows us to move the lower leg back and forth. A sesamoid bone, the patella (kneecap), lies at the front of the knee joint.

Lower leg

There are two bones in the lower leg—the tibia and the fibula. They are connected by strong fibers that allow the bones to rotate around each other. The tibia, on the inside of the leg, is the larger and stronger of the two bones and supports the body weight. The smaller, weaker fibula, on the outside of the leg, takes little of the body weight, but it does give strength to the ankle joint.

Foot

The tibia and fibula meet the talus (ankle bone) at a hinge joint at the top of the foot. The talus fits into the calcaneus (heel bone), which lies underneath it and supports it. Together with five more bones, the tarsals, these take the weight of the body. The talus acts as a lever, with major muscles attached to it via the Achilles tendon.

The long central part of the foot is made up from five **metatarsal** bones, and these are attached to the phalanges (toe bones). The arrangement of bones is similar to that in the hands, but the bones are more restricted and have much less freedom of movement than in the hand.

Flat feet

If the ligaments in the foot are weak, the bones may move apart. The talus drops down into the space and the shape of the arch collapses. This can usually be corrected by wearing a specially shaped insert (an orthotic) inside the shoe to support the bones.

Healthy bones

The bones of your legs and feet support the rest of your body and allow you to move around. As with the other bones in your body, you can help to keep them strong and healthy by exercising and eating a healthy diet. Protecting bones makes sense, too; wearing leg pads for sports like football and hockey can help to avoid injuries.

IN FOCUS: SHOCK ABSORBERS

The tarsals and metatarsals are arranged in the shape of an arch, keeping us stable when we stand. This arch also allows the foot to absorb shock when we walk and run. A running step may flatten the arch by 1–2 centimeters (0.5–1 inch), but it springs back into shape when the pressure is released.

What Can Go Wrong with My Bones?

This book has explained the different parts of the human skeleton, why it is important, and how it can be damaged by injury and illness. The table below summarizes some of the problems that can affect young people. It also gives information about treating each problem and tells you some of the ways you can prevent injury and illness.

Illness or injury	Cause	Symptoms	Prevention	Treatment
stress fracture of the shinbones	a repeated action that puts too much strain on particular bones. Running on a hard road can put pressure on the shinbones (tibia).	sharp pain in the shin. This can often be confused with shin splints, a pain in the shin that has similar causes but is less serious.	good running shoes that cushion the legs and prevent too much stress on the shins. The shoes that protect your shins best may not be the most expensive or fashionable ones.	the main treatment is to rest the affected area until the fracture has healed, which can take months. Exercise in a way that doesn't put weight on the area, like swimming.
rickets	lack of vitamin D or calcium in the diet, which prevents new bone tissue from being made	bones become weak, which causes them to bend—for example, leg bones become bent	make sure you are eating the right things. Calcium and vitamin D are both found in milk and other dairy products.	change of diet to include more calcium and vitamin D
sprained joints	joint gets overstretched or twisted too far—for example, if you trip and twist an ankle	joint is sore and you are unable to put pressure on it—for example, by walking	many joint problems can be prevented by warming up properly before exercising	the joint needs to be rested, preferably in a raised position. Ice will help to reduce swelling.
osteoarthritis	cartilage that cushions joints is worn away and not replaced. Main cause in young people is when joints, which are still developing, are overexercised or someone continues to play sports when injured.	joints are very painful when moved	don't push your body too hard. When your body is still developing, it is vulnerable when you put too much strain on joints like your knee joints. Don't use anabolic steroids.	medicines may be given to reduce inflammation. Rest followed by physiotherapy can help to strengthen damaged joints.
spinal problems and back pain	can be caused by poor posture when standing or sitting. This is also caused by lifting heavy objects and by carrying unbalanced loads.	muscle aches and weakened ligaments—for example in legs. In severe cases, the spine can become unusually curved.	stand up straight with weight distributed equally over both feet. Sit up straight in front of the TV or computer. Bend at the knees when lifting heavy objects.	improved posture and exercise and careful lifting and carrying

Many health problems can also be avoided by healthy behavior. This is called prevention. Exercising regularly and getting plenty of rest are important, as is eating a balanced diet. This is important in your teenage years, when your body is still developing.

Remember, if you think something is wrong with your body, you should always talk to a trained medical professional, like a doctor or school nurse. Regular medical checkups are an important part of maintaining a healthy body.

Find Out More

Books to read

Jakab, Cheryl. *Skeletal System (Our Body)*. Mankato, Minn.: Smart Apple Media, 2006.

Parker, Steve. *Move Your Body: Bones and Muscles (Body Talk)*. Chicago: Raintree, 2007.

Parker, Steve. *The Skeleton and Muscles (Our Bodies)*. Chicago: Raintree, 2004.

Websites to visit

http://kidshealth.org/teen/your_body/body_basics/bones_muscles_joints.html
  This website for young people has information about muscles, maintaining healthy and strong bones, and bone problems.

www.biology4kids.com/files/systems_skeletal.html
  This website offers information about bones and how they work.

www.kidport.com/RefLib/Science/HumanBody/BodyBones.htm
  This interactive website provides information about the human skeleton.

Glossary

antibiotics drugs used to fight infections. They destroy microorganisms such as bacteria or fungi but are not effective against viruses.

bacteria type of microorganism

bone marrow soft tissue at the center of some bones, where blood cells may be produced and fat may be stored

bursa soft sac inside some joints that acts as a shock absorber

cancerous to do with cancer

cartilage strong, flexible material that protects bones

cervical to do with the neck

clavicle collarbone

coccyx tailbone

compact bone strong, hard material that forms part of a bone

cranium dome of skull

dislocate move a bone out of its normal position

femur thighbone

fibula shinbone (smaller)

fracture broken bone

friction force that occurs when two surfaces rub together

gene part of every cell that contains genetic information

hormone chemical made in the body. Hormones travel around the body in the blood and affect organs and tissues in a variety of ways.

humerus upper arm bone

immune system body's natural defense against disease and infection

inflammation swelling and tenderness of a joint or other tissue

intercostal between the ribs

ligament strong band of fibers that hold joints together

lumbar to do with the lower back

mass amount of material that something is made of

membrane thin covering layer of tissue

metacarpal hand bone

metatarsal foot bone

microorganism tiny living thing that can only be seen under a microscope

mineral one of a number of chemicals needed by the body in small amounts

occupational therapist person who helps a patient to recover after injury or illness by helping the patient perform appropriate exercises

orthopedic branch of medicine specializing in bones and joints

ossicle one of the three tiny bones inside the ear

osteoblast cell that is involved in formation of bone tissue

osteoclast cell that breaks down bone tissue

osteocyte bone cell

paralysis inability to move part of the body

pectoral girdle scapulae and clavicles

pelvic girdle pelvis, sacrum, and coccyx

phalanges bones of fingers and toes

protein complex chemical that is a component of many of the body's structures

radius lower arm (smaller bone)

rigid stiff and inflexible

sacral to do with the sacrum

sacrum vertebra forming back of pelvic girdle

scapula shoulder blade

sinus hollow space within a bone

speech therapy treatment to help people with speech and language problems

spinal cord bundle of nerves that runs within the spinal column

spleen large abdominal organ involved in the formation and destruction of blood cells

splint strong, rigid frame used to support and immobilize an injured bone

spongy bone mesh-like structure at the center of some bones

sternum breastbone

steroid human-made drug that is similar to some chemicals found naturally in the body

tendon strong fibers that connect muscles to bones

thoracic to do with the chest

tibia shinbone (larger)

tissue different types of cell that work together to do one job

tumor swelling caused by abnormal growth of new cells

ulna lower arm (larger bone)

vertebra one of the bones of the spine

vitamin one of a number of chemicals that are needed by the body in very small amounts

Index

accessory bones **9**
ankle **4, 8, 9, 19, 22, 28, 43**
arm **40–41**
arthritis **26–27, 28, 44**
astronauts **7**

babies and children **4, 9, 10, 17, 27, 35, 37**
back pain **34, 44**
bacterial infections **16**
blood cells **11, 12–13, 15**
bone cells **10**
bone marrow **4–5, 11, 12–13**
    transplants **13**
bone tissue **4, 7, 10, 15, 16, 17**
bones
    broken **14–15, 16, 23, 34, 39**
    healthy bones **6–7, 43**
    illness and injury **14–17, 22–27, 34–35, 39, 41, 44**
    structure and composition **10–11**
    types of bone **4, 8–9**
brittle bone disease **17**
bursae **21, 24**

calcium **4, 6, 7, 10, 16, 17**
carpal tunnel syndrome **41**
carpals/metacarpals **9, 41**
carrying, bending, and lifting **32–33, 44**
cartilage **11, 15, 18, 19, 20, 21, 24, 26, 28, 31, 34, 38**
chest surgery **39**
clavicles (collarbones) **5, 15, 38, 40**
cleft lip and palate **37**
coccyx **30, 42**
compact bone **11, 15**
cranial bones **9, 11, 36, 37**

diet **6, 16**
discs **31, 34**
dislocation **23, 29, 42**

elbow joint **18, 23, 40**
exercise **7, 16, 21, 33**

facial bones **4, 9, 36–37**
femur (thighbone) **4, 5, 8, 11, 12, 16, 19, 21, 24, 29, 42**
fibula **5, 14, 24, 43**
flat bones **4, 8, 9, 11, 12, 38**
flat feet **43**
fontanelles **37**

foot **9, 43**
fractures **14–15, 16, 23, 34, 39, 44**

hand **9, 40, 41**
hip joint **19, 21, 26, 28, 29**
hormones **12, 16**
"housemaid's knee" **23**
humerus (upper arm bone) **5, 8, 18, 19, 23, 40**

inflammation **23, 27, 37**
irregular bones **8, 9, 11, 36**

joints **4, 18–29, 36**
    ball-and-socket joints **19, 40, 42**
    condyloid joints **19**
    fixed and gliding joints **19, 20, 41**
    hinge joints **18, 43**
    pivot joints **19**
    problems and injuries **22–27**
    replacements **28–29**
    saddle joints **19, 41**
    synovial joints **20–21**

knee joint **18, 20, 21, 24–25, 26, 27, 28, 29, 43**

leg **42–43**
leukemia **13**
ligaments **4, 18, 19, 21, 22, 23, 24–25, 40, 41, 42**
long bones **4, 8, 12**
lumbar vertebrae **30, 33**

minerals **4, 6, 7, 10, 16, 17, 37**
muscles **4, 7, 8, 39, 40, 42, 43**

nerves **31, 34, 35**

ossicles **4, 8**
osteoarthritis **26, 27, 28, 44**
osteoblasts **10, 11, 15**
osteoclasts **10, 15**
osteocytes **10**
osteomalacia **17**
osteomyelitis **16**
osteoporosis **16**
osteosarcomas **17**

patellae (kneecaps) **8, 9, 24, 25, 43**
pectoral girdle **32, 40**
pelvic girdle **4, 5, 12, 19, 20, 29, 30, 42**
phalanges **41, 43**

phosphorus **4, 6**
posture **33, 35, 44**

radius **5, 18, 40–41**
rheumatoid arthritis **26, 27**
ribcage **4, 5, 38–39**
ribs **9, 12, 38, 39**
RICE treatment **22**
rickets **17, 35, 44**
"runner's knee" **25**

sacrum **30, 42**
scapulae (shoulder blades) **5, 9, 40**
scoliosis **35**
sesamoid bones **8, 9, 43**
shinbones **15, 44**
short bones **4, 8, 9, 11**
shoulder joint **19, 23, 28, 29, 40**
sinuses **11, 37**
skeleton **4–5**
skull **4, 5, 8, 9, 11, 19, 20, 34, 36–37**
spina bifida **35**
spinal cord **4, 8, 30, 31, 34, 35**
spine **4, 5, 30–35**
    caring for **32–33**
    curvature of **35**
    problems and injuries **34–35, 44**
    vertebrae **8, 9, 19, 30–31, 33, 34, 35, 38, 40**
spongy bone **10, 11, 15, 16**
sports injuries **7, 15, 22, 23, 27, 33, 43**
sprains **22, 44**
sternum (breastbone) **9, 12, 20, 38, 40**
sutural bones **9, 36**
synovial fluid and membrane **18, 19, 20, 21, 26**

tarsals/metatarsals **8, 9, 43**
tendons **4, 9, 21, 24, 41**
"tennis elbow" **23, 40**
thoracic vertebrae **30, 35, 38**
tibia **5, 14, 24, 43**
tumors **17**

ulna **5, 18, 40–41**

vertebrae **8, 9, 19, 30–31, 33, 34, 35, 38, 40**
vitamins **6, 16, 17**

whiplash injury **34**
wrist **4, 9, 19, 28, 41**